RAIL ROVER
WEST MIDLANDS RANGER

Andrew Cole

AMBERLEY

First published 2018

Amberley Publishing
The Hill, Stroud
Gloucestershire, GL5 4EP

www.amberley-books.com

Copyright © Andrew Cole, 2018

ISBN 978 1 4456 7947 1 (print)
ISBN 978 1 4456 7948 8 (ebook)

British Library Cataloguing in Publication Data.
A catalogue record for this book is available from
the British Library.

Origination by Amberley Publishing.
Printed in the UK.

Introduction

Welcome to this book, which covers some of the places that are to be found within the boundaries of the West Midlands Rail Rover. The rover covers the lines from as far north as Crewe, right down to Northampton, and as far west as Hereford.

This album of photographs aims to show some of the different types of motive power and workings that could be found along these routes. The book starts off at its northern point of Crewe, which in days gone by was always a fantastic place to visit, as not only were there vast amounts of locos to be seen at the station and depots, where you could spend hours just watching the comings and goings, but there were also the eagerly anticipated visits to Crewe Works.

We then work our way south along the West Coast Main Line, visiting places such as Stafford and Nuneaton. Both of these two places are superb to visit; indeed, both are as busy today as they were back in the 1980s, when I first started taking an interest.

The book then takes a brief detour into the West Midlands itself, featuring Wolverhampton and also showing many of the different classes of locomotives that could be found at Bescot. There is a brief tour of Birmingham, including some scenes at Washwood Heath and Water Orton, before heading back to the West Coast Main Line, visiting Rugby and Northampton. Finally, there are a couple of shots taken at Hereford.

This album hopes to show some of the different varieties of locomotives and workings that were to be seen from the 1980s onwards at these locations, many of which are now just a memory. It also gives a more up to date look at the same locations, showing how the traffic and locos have changed over the years.

Compiling this book has been quite an eye opener for me, as it reminded me just how much traffic was on my doorstep, being from Birmingham, and just how much traffic has been unfortunately lost over time. It also shows just how much the different types of traction have changed, from the humble shunter through to the modern APT, and how the different liveries carried have evolved.

This book doesn't aim to be a complete historical record of every location to be visited within the Day Ranger boundaries, but more of a collection of some of my favourite photographs taken over the years, accompanying my brother and late father.

I hope you enjoy browsing through this book, and hopefully it will rekindle some memories for you, as it has done for me in compiling it. Hopefully, having seen some of the places you can visit, you might be encouraged to visit yourselves, as there are still some fascinating things to be seen.

Crewe

No. 08921, 13 January 1993

No. 08921 (D4151) is seen at Crewe while shunting a small rake of two-axle diesel tank wagons. This used to be an everyday scene throughout British Rail days, with most depots receiving their fuel by rail. No. 08921 has recently been saved from scrapping at European Metal Recycling, Kingsbury.

No. 25173, 31 August 1984

No. 25173 (D7523) is seen at Crewe while carrying British Rail blue livery. At this time the vast majority of locomotives carried the standard blue livery, with just a few depots applying local variations. No. 25173 was lucky enough to be preserved, and is today based at the Epping & Ongar Railway.

No. 25302, 31 August 1984

No. 25302 (D7652) runs through Crewe station with an overhead line electrification maintenance train, including a cable drum carrier. This shot was taken before Crewe station was remodelled in 1985, which resulted in a higher speed on the through main lines.

No. 31119, 2 November 1993

No. 31119 (D5537) arrives at Crewe while hauling a single Mk 1 RMB Miniature Buffet coach. At this time, the Class 31s were used on such empty coaching stock moves between depots. No. 31119 carries Civil Engineers 'Dutch' livery, and it would eventually be preserved at the Embsay & Bolton Abbey Railway.

No. 31420, 13 January 1993

No. 31420 (D5591, No. 31172) arrives at Crewe while hauling Mk 3 DVT No. 82149 into the station. No. 31420 was renumbered from 31172 when it was fitted with ETH equipment, and is seen carrying InterCity Mainline livery. No. 31420 would be scrapped by C. F. Booth, Rotherham, in 2007.

No. 31429, 27 March 1993

No. 31429 (D5699, No. 31269) is seen condemned on the Crewe depot scrap line, along with Class 47s Nos 47460 and 47512. No. 31429 was renumbered from 31269, and it would be scrapped the following year by Booth Roe Metals, Rotherham.

No. 33014, 2 April 1983

No. 33014 (D6522) is seen departing Crewe for Cardiff Central. The Class 33s were used on these diagrams in the early 1980s, and they were always nice to see this far north. No. 33014 would be withdrawn with collision damage, and was scrapped at Eastleigh in 1986.

No. 33030, 31 August 1984

No. 33030 (D6548) waits to depart from Crewe with a service to Cardiff Central, complete with unseasonable snowploughs. The large building in the left background is Rail House, which was owned by British Rail at the time. No. 33030 is currently owned by West Coast Railways, and is stored at Carnforth.

No. 33043, 31 August 1984

No. 33043 (D6561) is seen unloading its passengers, having arrived at Crewe from Cardiff Central. The Class 33s were always sought-after on a visit to Crewe, as they were such a long way from their normal operating area. No. 33043 would eventually be scrapped by M. C. Metals, Glasgow, in 1991.

No. 37108, 1 June 1996

No. 37108 (D6808, No. 37325) is seen being hauled through Crewe station by classmate No. 37242. No. 37108 carries unbranded Trainload Freight livery, and it would be lucky enough to be preserved. Today it can be found at the Crewe Heritage Centre, having spent many years in service in Scotland.

No. 37129, 13 December 1986
No. 37129 (D6829, No. 37669) is seen stabled round the back of Crewe station. It was waiting to be tripped round to the nearby Crewe Works, where it would be refurbished and emerge as No. 37669. It is seen carrying BR blue livery, complete with Highland Stag sticker.

No. 37223, 13 January 1993
No. 37223 (D6923) is seen stabled on the through road near Platform 12 at Crewe while carrying Trainload Coal livery, which is appropriate as it is on a domestic coal working. These services have ceased to operate on the network today, as have the majority of power station coal workings.

No. 37407, 11 October 1993

No. 37407 (D6605, No. 37305) arrives at Crewe station while carrying InterCity Mainline livery, complete with the name *Loch Long*. No. 37407 is working a Birmingham New Street to Holyhead passenger working, which was in the hands of Class 37/4s at the time.

No. 37414, 27 March 1993

No. 37414 (D6987, No. 37287) is seen at Crewe having just been repainted into Regional Railways livery, and is carrying the name *Cathays C&W Works 1846–1993*. This was one of the first Class 37 locomotives to receive this livery, and it would be scrapped by T. J. Thompson, Stockton, in 2007.

No. 37421, 1 June 1996

No. 37421 (D6967, No. 37267) *The Kingsman* is seen making a station call at Crewe with a Regional Railways working to Holyhead. The Regional Railways livery and miniature snowploughs suited this class well, and No. 37421 is still in use today, working for Colas Rail Freight.

No. 37429, 1 March 1993

No. 37429 (D6600, No. 37300) departs Crewe with a Regional Railways passenger working to Birmingham New Street. This loco carries Trainload Construction livery, and the scar on the bodywork is where the name *Eisteddfod Genedlaethol* has been removed. No. 37429 was scrapped by European Metal Recycling, Kingsbury, in 2008.

No. 37604, 1 June 1996

No. 37604 (D6707, Nos 37007 and 37506) arrives at Crewe with Pathfinder Tours' Cumbrian Coaster Railtour. This tour started at Bristol Temple Meads with EPS Nos 37604 and 37611 in charge, before handing over to Nos 20301, 302 and 303 at Crewe.

No. 40122, 2 June 1984

No. 40122 (D200) is seen stabled at Crewe having arrived with the Midland Executive Railtour from Derby. This tour had started at London Waterloo behind Nos 73114 and 73140, and also included Nos 56031, 33060 and 73125 on the return leg. No. 40122 was preserved by the National Railway Museum, as it was the first Class 40 locomotive built.

No. 40150, 10 May 1986

No. 40150 (D350) stands condemned in the Crewe Works scrap line along with at least nine classmates. This was always an area of the Works that was eagerly anticipated during a visit, as it would probably be the last time some of these huge locomotives would be seen.

No. 43168, 22 March 1986

No. 43168 departs Crewe station while still carrying blue and grey livery, including the Mk 3 coaching stock. InterCity Executive livery had started to be applied to the Class 43 locomotives at this point, but No. 43168 had yet to be repainted.

No. 43172, 18 June 1990

No. 43172 is seen departing Crewe station while carrying InterCity Swallow livery. This was the livery applied to all the HST train sets during this time, and today No. 43172 is still at work on the Great Western, carrying the name *Harry Patch The Last Survivor of the Trenches*.

No. 45053, 2 June 1984

No. 45053 (D76) stands condemned at Crewe Works. The works at Crewe was always a great place to visit, with in excess of 100 locos on site in various conditions, from new build through to locos waiting dismantling. No. 45053 would survive another four years, being broken up in 1988.

No. 45112, 17 January 2002

No. 45112 (D61) is seen departing from one of the south bay platforms at Crewe. This loco had recently returned to main-line use, and it still carries its impressive *The Royal Army Ordnance Corps* nameplates.

No. 47329, 20 August 1993

No. 47329 (D1810, No. 57011) is seen passing through Crewe station while carrying Civil Engineers 'Dutch' livery while on a ballast working, which consists of a now redundant rake of Dogfish wagons. No. 47329 would go on to be rebuilt as No. 57011 for Freightliner.

No. 47467, 20 October 1996

No. 47467 (D1593) is seen stabled on Crewe Diesel depot while carrying large logo livery. At this time, Crewe were responsible for maintaining the RES fleet of Class 47 locomotives, and as can be seen, most of the fleet carried either Parcels livery or RES livery, but with a few exceptions, including No. 47467.

No. 47521, 31 August 1984

No. 47521 (D1104) is seen at Crewe station having just emerged from an overhaul at the nearby Works. Most locomotives would make their way to the Diesel depot for refueling after being released from the Works, and then move on to their home depot. No. 47521 would be scrapped at Crewe Works following collision damage in 1995.

No. 47586, 23 November 1985

No. 47586 (D1623, Nos 47042 and 47676) is seen waiting its turn for attention at Crewe Works. This was the first of an additional eighty Class 47 conversions, due to an extra requirement for ETH-fitted locomotives. No. 47586 was converted from 47042, and would eventually be scrapped by Booth Roe Metals, Rotherham, in 1998, carrying the number 47676.

No. 47612, 14 February 1987

No. 47612 (D1655, Nos 47080, 47838 and 47779) is seen having arrived at Crewe while carrying original InterCity livery. This was one of the original Western Region named Class 47s, and indeed at the time still retained its *Titan* nameplates. This loco went through various renumberings, eventually becoming 47779 in the RES fleet.

No. 47636, 27 March 1993

No. 47636 (D1920, Nos 47243 and 47777) is seen stabled outside Crewe depot. This loco had recently been through an overhaul, in which it had lost its large logo livery and had gained a coat of RES red. It also changed its name from *Sir John De Graeme* to *Restored*. It would eventually be renumbered to 47777.

No. 47712, 12 June 2008

No. 47712 (D1948, No. 47505) is seen entering one of the south bays at Crewe while carrying Direct Rail Services livery, complete with *Pride of Carlisle* nameplates. This loco has since been preserved at the nearby Crewe Heritage Centre, and has been reunited with its *Lady Diana Spencer* nameplates.

No. 47722, 10 June 1999

No. 47722 (D1599, Nos 47027 and 47558) is seen on one of the through roads at Crewe while carrying RES livery. At this time there was still an incredible amount of Parcels traffic to be seen on the network. Today, unfortunately, almost all of it has been lost. No. 47722 carries the name *The Queen Mother*.

No. 47785, 27 May 1998

No. 47785 (D1909, Nos 47232, 47665 and 47820) *Fiona Castle* is seen stabled at Crewe depot while carrying EWS maroon livery. This view shows what at the time was an everyday scene at Crewe, with plenty of locomotives stabled ready to work Parcels trains in the evening. Crewe was always a great station to visit, with plenty of movements on and off the depot all day long.

No. 47789, 20 October 1996

No. 47789 (D1925, Nos 47248, 47616 and 47671) is seen having just come off the stabling sidings at Crewe, and is ready to leave the depot. This loco carries the name *Lindisfarne*, and is another to have undergone various renumberings throughout its career.

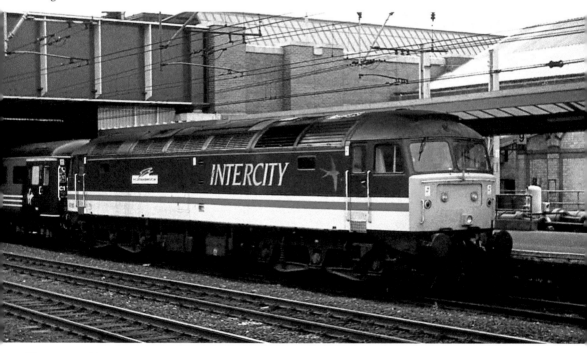

No. 47810, 24 May 1998

No. 47810 (D1924, Nos 47247 and 47655) is seen at Crewe at the head of a Virgin Trains Cross Country passenger working. This shot was taken at the dawn of privatisation, with the carriages having already been repainted. No. 47810 still retains its InterCity Swallow livery, although it has gained the attractive *Porterbrook* nameplate.

No. 47817, 7 August 1996

No. 47817 (D1611, Nos 47032, 47662 and 57311) departs Crewe with a passenger working towards Manchester Piccadilly. No. 47817 carries the livery of owner Porterbrook, and was one of two Class 47s to carry this livery, the other being No. 47807. No. 87002 also carried a different version of the livery. No. 47817 would be rebuilt as No. 57311 for Virgin Trains West Coast.

No. 47850, 27 August 1995

No. 47850 (D1744, Nos 47151 and 47648) is seen stabled round the back of Crewe station, carrying severe collision damage. It received the damage at Longsight when it collided with No. 90139. This area of the station is where locos were stored before being tripped round to the nearby Works. No. 47850 was never repaired, and was broken up at Crewe Works in 1997.

No. 56311, 24 June 2008

No. 56311 (No. 56057) is seen waiting for the road at Crewe while carrying plain grey livery. This loco had not long been renumbered from 56057, and this view shows that there was still some variety to be seen at Crewe, but not as much as in years gone by.

No. 57304, 24 June 2008

No. 57304 (D1639, Nos 47055, 47652 and 47807) arrives at Crewe while hauling a Virgin Trains Class 390 unit from Holyhead. For a short while, these services were diesel-hauled to and from Crewe, but today Class 221 Voyager DEMUs operate these services. No. 57304 carries the name *Thunderbirds Gordon Tracy*.

No. 66099, 12 June 2008

No. 66099 is seen passing through Crewe on the Down fast with a rake of empty container wagons. This view shows what today's motive power is at Crewe, with mainly foreign-built Class 66s dominating.

No. 66542, 30 October 2012

No. 66542 is seen at Crewe as part of a five-loco light engine move. All the locos are operated by Freightliner, and the consist includes a pair of Class 66 locomotives and three Class 86 electric locomotives including a Class 86 carrying PowerHaul livery. All five carry Freightliner green livery.

No. 73006, 21 August 1994

No. 73006 (E6006, Nos 73906 and 73967) is seen on display at Crewe Basford Hall open day, 1994. The open days held here were always great to attend, with plenty of room to space out the displays. No. 73006 carries Merseyrail livery, as at the time it was used on Sandite duties on the system. Today it has been rebuilt as No. 73967, and is in use in Scotland on Caledonian Sleeper workings.

No. 81008, 13 December 1986

No. 81008 (E3010) is seen at Crewe while double-heading a freight with No. 87032. The amount of different varieties of traffic at Crewe during this time was huge, as can be seen with the Travelling Post Office (TPO) in the background, as well as the Class 81-headed freight. No. 81008 would be scrapped by Coopers Metals in 1991.

No. 82003, 27 March 1993

No. 82003 (E3049) stands in the scrap lines at Crewe Electric depot. This loco had been withdrawn for ten years, and was used as a source of spares for the other two Class 82 locomotives that were used for empty coaching stock (ECS) moves out of London Euston. No. 82003 would be scrapped three months later by Booth Roe Metals, Rotherham.

No. 85007, 25 January 1986

No. 85007 (E3062, No. 85112) departs Crewe with a southbound TPO working. Being at the centre of the West Coast Main Line, Crewe always had plenty of AC electric locomotives passing through on various passenger and freight workings. No. 85007 was eventually renumbered to 85112.

No. 85020, 14 February 1987

No. 85020 (E3075) is seen having arrived at Crewe with a container working. Today, most of the freight workings use the station avoiding line to enter Basford Hall yard. No. 85020 was scrapped by M. C. Metals, Glasgow, in 1993.

No. 85026, 23 November 1985

No. 85026 (E3081) works north through Platform 6 at Crewe with a container working. Crewe was always a good place to see electric locomotives, as the nearby Works was their main place for overhauls. No. 85026 was another Class 85 that was scrapped by M. C. Metals, Glasgow, in 1993.

No. 85103 26 July 1990

No. 85103 (E3065, No. 85010) passes light engine through Crewe as a classmate looks on in the background. The loco had been renumbered from 85010, and, as can be seen, BR blue livery was still carried by a lot of locomotives at this time.

No. 86007, 22 March 1986

No. 86007 (E3176, Nos 86407 and 86607) is seen moving onto the stabling point at Crewe while still carrying blue livery. No. 86007 is still in use with Freightliner today, although it has been renumbered to 86607, and the sidings in the background are used to stable coaches.

No. 86103, 31 August 1984

No. 86103 (E3143) departs Crewe with a southbound passenger working. This locomotive was one of just three in the Class 86/1 sub-group, with the main difference being that they rode on Class 87 bogies, as can be seen. No. 86103 carries the name *Andre Chapelon*, and was scrapped at Immingham Railfreight Terminal in 2002.

No. 86207, 14 February 1987

No. 86207 (E3179) *City of Lichfield* departs Crewe with a passenger working. I always looked forward to visiting Crewe, both the station and Works, for the vast amount of traffic and locomotives that were to be seen at both locations.

No. 86242, 1 June 1996

No. 86242 (E3138) is seen arriving at Crewe with a rake of InterCity-liveried Mk 3 carriages. This would be the standard West Coast Main Line formation for many years, with either a Class 86, 87 or 90 leading, until the introduction of the Class 390 Pendolino units by Virgin Trains.

No. 86250, 27 October 1984

No. 86250 (E3189, No. 0450 002–5) is seen running light engine through Crewe. This was taken before the station was remodelled, which made the layout a lot simpler, and also increased the line speed through the station. No. 86250 carries the name *The Glasgow Herald*, and is today in use in Hungary, working for Floyd.

No. 86408, 22 March 1986

No. 86408 (E3180, Nos 86008, 86608 and 86501) departs Crewe with a southbound passenger working. This was more likely a Cross Country working towards Birmingham judging by the Mk 2 carriages. No. 86408 carries InterCity livery, and would go on to be renumbered as 86501, before being renumbered back to 86608, and works today for Freightliner.

No. 92005, 21 August 1994

No. 92005 (No. 472005) is seen on display at one of the hugely impressive Crewe Basford Hall open days. At the time No. 92005 carried the name *Mozart*, but it has since been exported to Romania, and today carries the name *Emil Cioran*.

No. 92007, 15 October 1994

No. 92007 *Schubert* is seen on display at Crewe Electric depot open day, 1994. These locomotives had not long entered traffic at this time, and they were split between three different operators, with No. 92007 carrying a BR logo, whereas No. 92006, behind, carries French SNCF markings. The other operator was EPS, with the intention of using their locomotives on passenger services. In the end, all the locomotives were used in a common pool.

No. 92018, 10 March 2015

No. 92018 is seen stabled in one of the south bays at Crewe. This had just been released from an overhaul at Brush, Loughborough, for use on overnight Caledonian Sleeper workings out of London Euston. This was originally one of the French-operated Class 92 locomotives, and carried the name *Stendhal*.

No. 92025, 27 August 1995

No. 92025 (No. 88025) *Oscar Wilde* is seen on display at Crewe Basford Hall open day, 1995. At this particular open day, there was a huge number of these locomotives on display. Today, No. 92025 can be found working in Bulgaria, carrying the number 88025.

No. 92028, 24 July 2017

No. 92028 is seen at Crewe while carrying GBRf livery. A large number of this class of locomotives are stored awaiting work today. No. 92028 was another French example, and was named *Saint-Saens*.

No. 46155, 23 August 1961

No. 46155 (6155) *The Lancer* is seen outside Crewe Works in 1961. This Royal Scot would have another three years of life left before being condemned in 1964. It was eventually scrapped by Arnott Young, Troon, in 1965.

No. 150237, 27 March 1993

No. 150237 is seen departing Crewe with a Regional Railways service to Nottingham. Despite its size, there were not too many DMU services that used Crewe at the time. Today, No. 150237 works for Arriva Trains Wales, based in Cardiff, and the Crewe to Nottingham services terminate at Derby and are operated by East Midlands Trains.

No. 325001, 30 March 1995

No. 325001 is seen at Crewe having not long been released from Litchurch Lane, Derby, following construction. There were originally sixteen of these units built for express Parcels services, but today only fifteen are in use, with No. 325010 having been scrapped.

No. 325007, 24 July 2017

No. 325007 is seen at Crewe, showing the difference in livery between the previous photograph and the livery these units carry today. These units are still in use carrying Parcels traffic, but they only have a handful of diagrams and are mainly used in twelve-car formations.

No. 370006, 31 August 1984

No. 370006 departs Crewe with a southbound passenger working. At this time there were just a handful of APT workings on the network, as there were only six half sets built, with a couple of spare cars, and it was always special to see one out working.

No. 370007, 31 August 1984

No. 370007 is seen on the rear of the same train as the previous photograph. I only ever saw these trains working twice – this one at Crewe and one set at Nuneaton.

Stafford

No. 37422, 20 August 1993

No. 37422 (D6966, No. 37266) *Robert F. Fairlie Locomotive Engineer 1831–1885* departs Stafford with a Regional Railways working from Birmingham New Street to Holyhead. This shot was taken before the Royal Mail platform was built on the wasteland behind; however, with the loss in Parcels traffic, the platform was only used for a short while.

No. 47348, 28 May 1998

No. 47348 (D1829) *St Christopher's Railway Home* is seen at Stafford hauling No. 92015 *D. H. Lawrence* from Dollands Moor to Crewe Electric depot. This shot was taken at the time when the Class 92 locomotives were hauled to and from Crewe for repairs, rather than working up on their own.

No. 47376, 28 May 1998

No. 47376 (D1895) works a northbound container working through Stafford. Stafford was always a great place to visit for freight workings, as many were seen due to the through traffic passing through the station that used the avoiding line at Crewe. Stafford is where the West Coast Main Line splits from the line towards Bescot. No. 47376 carries the name *Freightliner 1995*, and is today preserved at the Gloucestershire & Warwickshire Railway.

No. 47536, 20 August 1993

No. 47536 (D1655) passes through Stafford on the Down fast with a short Parcels working, consisting of just two Royal Mail-liveried BG vans. No. 47536 carries the unofficial name of *Solario*, and was scrapped by C. F. Booth, Rotherham, in 2005.

No. 47640, 20 August 1993

No. 47640 (D1921, No. 47244) double-heads a southbound Parcels working through Stafford along with No. 86426. Stafford was also a great place to see Parcels traffic, especially after the dedicated platform was built. No. 47640 carries the name *University of Strathclyde*, and is today preserved at the Battlefield Line.

No. 47853, 6 March 2002

No. 47853 (D1733, Nos 47141 and 47614) makes a station call at Stafford with a Virgin Trains Cross Country working to Manchester Piccadilly. This locomotive had been repainted back into its unique XP64 blue livery, which it carried in the 1960s as a precursor to Rail blue. The Royal Mail platform can be seen in the background.

No. 304037, 20 August 1993

No. 304037 departs Stafford while carrying Regional Railways livery, which was only carried by a small handful of these units. The train is working to Liverpool Lime Street, and is seen just before the Class 323 units were introduced onto this route. The Class 304 units on this route were superb to ride on, especially between Stafford and Crewe, with plenty of scope to stretch their legs.

No. 309627, 28 May 1998

No. 309627 arrives at Stafford with a North West Trains working from Manchester Piccadilly to Birmingham International. Regional Railways inherited seven of these units out of storage and used them for a number of years around Manchester before they passed to North West Trains. They were all taken out of use in 2000.

No. 322484, 28 May 1998

No. 322484 passes Stafford on one of the short-lived North West Trains workings from London Euston to Manchester Airport. NWT had two of these units painted in their livery for these services, although they would only be used for a couple of years before passing back to West Anglia Great Northern.

Nuneaton

No. 08928, 29 August 1989

No. 08928 (D4158) passes Nuneaton while carrying red stripe Railfreight livery. Nuneaton used to have a Class 08 to shunt the yards, which were behind No. 08928, but by the time this photograph was taken the yard had been lifted. Today, a supermarket has been built on the site.

No. 25285, 20 February 1985

No. 25285 (D7635) speeds a southbound Parcels working through Nuneaton on the Up fast. This view shows some of the diverse traffic that could be seen at Nuneaton, and indeed both Parcels and Coal traffic have all but ceased to be carried on the network today.

No. 31234, 22 April 1987

No. 31234 (D5661) hauls a mixed rake of Catfish and Dogfish ballast wagons through Platform 1 at Nuneaton. Nuneaton was always another great place for a variety of traffic, and it is still so today, as it is where the busy line from Birmingham to Leicester bisects the West Coast Main Line.

No. 45003, 3 April 1985

No. 45003 (D133) is seen light engine at Nuneaton. All the sidings in the background have since been lifted. Nuneaton was always a nice place to go, as it was not far from home and it was the closest station on the West Coast Main Line for us to visit.

No. 47061, 3 April 1985

No. 47061 (D1645, Nos 47649 and 47830) awaits the road at Nuneaton with a rake of bogie oil tank wagons. This could possibly have originated from the oil depot at Bedworth, which is just a few miles down the line towards Coventry. No. 47061 is still in use today with Freightliner, although it now carries the number 47830.

No. 47243, 3 April 1985

No. 47243 (D1920, Nos 47636 and 47777) is seen light engine at Nuneaton. At this time British Rail blue livery still held strong on many locomotives, with just a few starting to carry InterCity and Railfreight grey. No. 47243 would carry a few different numbers, including 47636, and was based in Scotland for many years.

No. 57312, 13 August 2005

No. 57312 (D1811, Nos 47330 and 47390) *Thunderbirds The Hood* is seen at Nuneaton while waiting for a Class 390 Pendolino to arrive from London Euston. The Class 57 would then couple up to the Class 390 and haul it towards Birmingham New Street via Whitacre Junction. This view shows the supermarket that was built on the former engineers yard in the background.

No. 57313, 13 August 2005

No. 57313 (D1890, No. 47371) *Thunderbirds Tracy Island* arrives at Nuneaton while hauling Class 390 No. 390043 from Birmingham New Street. This type of working had been occurring for many years on the occasion when the line between Rugby and Coventry was closed. This view shows the new line that was built to the right for trains from Leicester to Birmingham in order to avoid conflicting moves across the West Coast Main Line.

No. 66614, 13 August 2005

No. 66614 runs light engine through Nuneaton while carrying Freightliner livery. This view shows the type of locomotive that can commonly be found working through Nuneaton today.

No. 67004, 13 August 2005

No. 67004 is seen arriving at Nuneaton with the Northern Belle rake of Pullman coaches. The Class 67 locomotives had been introduced to work Parcels traffic, but by this time a lot of their work had ceased to be carried, and a use for them on charter traffic was found. No. 67004 carries the name *Post Haste*.

No. 81019, 3 April 1985

No. 81019 (E3022) brings a rake of Mk 1 carriages to a halt at Nuneaton. This shot was taken at the time before the Class 90 locomotives had been introduced on the West Coast Main Line, and almost any type of AC electric could turn up on any type of working. No. 81019, like many of its classmates, was scrapped by Coopers Metals in 1991.

No. 85031, 3 April 1985

No. 85031 (E3086) is seen making a station call at Nuneaton. This view was taken on the same day as the previous shot, and goes to show that any available loco could be seen on the West Coast Main Line. No. 85031 would be scrapped by M. C. Metals, Glasgow, in 1992.

No. 85035, 22 April 1987

No. 85035 (E3090, No. 85109) works a southbound passenger working through Nuneaton. Of note are the two BG brake coaches, as most formation only had the one. This shot was taken before the introduction of the Mk 3 driving van trailers, which eliminated the BG coaches, and also the need for locos to be coupled and uncoupled at terminal stations.

No. 86260, 22 April 1987

No. 86260 (E3144, Nos 86702, 87702 and 85002) hauls a mixed bag of Mk 1, 2 and 3 carriages through Nuneaton. This was during the transitional period when British Rail was replacing the blue and grey livery with InterCity. No. 86260 carries the name *Driver Wallace Oakes G. C.*, and can today be found working in Bulgaria for Bulmarket, carrying the number 85002 (having previously carried 87702).

No. 86432, 22 April 1987

No. 86432 (E3148, Nos 86032 and 86632) departs from Nuneaton with a northbound passenger working. This locomotive is still in use on the West Coast Main Line today, working for Freightliner and carrying the number 86632.

No. 53210, 3 April 1985

No. 53210 (50210) departs Nuneaton with a working from Norwich to Birmingham New Street. At this time, these services used either a Norwich-based DMU or a Class 31 and carriages, although a Stratford-based Class 47 could also sometimes be seen. Class 156 Super Sprinter units would take over these services from 1988 onwards.

No. 55034, 29 August 1989

No. 55034 is seen arriving at Nuneaton with a stopping service from Stafford. Today, these services are incorporated into the London Euston to Crewe services, and No. 55034 has recently finished its main-line career with Chiltern Railways.

No. 303067, 26 October 1982

No. 303067 departs Nuneaton, heading towards Stafford. A handful of these units were transferred from Glasgow to Longsight for use around Manchester, although a few did spread their wings south to Nuneaton and Rugby.

No. 370003, 3 April 1985

No. 370003 speeds through Nuneaton with a working to London Euston. This was only the second time I had seen an APT in action, and No. 370007 was on the rear. Today, the driving car from No. 370003, No. 48103, can be found at the Crewe Heritage Centre.

Wolverhampton

No. 08714, 15 March 2004

No. 08714 (D3881) is seen on pilot duty at Wolverhampton Steel Terminal. This terminal is still active today, although there is no longer a Class 08 based there, with the arriving main-line locomotive doing the required shunting.

No. 66149, 25 March 2013

No. 66149 is seen at a snowy Wolverhampton Steel Terminal. This view shows the current type of motive power used on the vast majority of freight trains in use today.

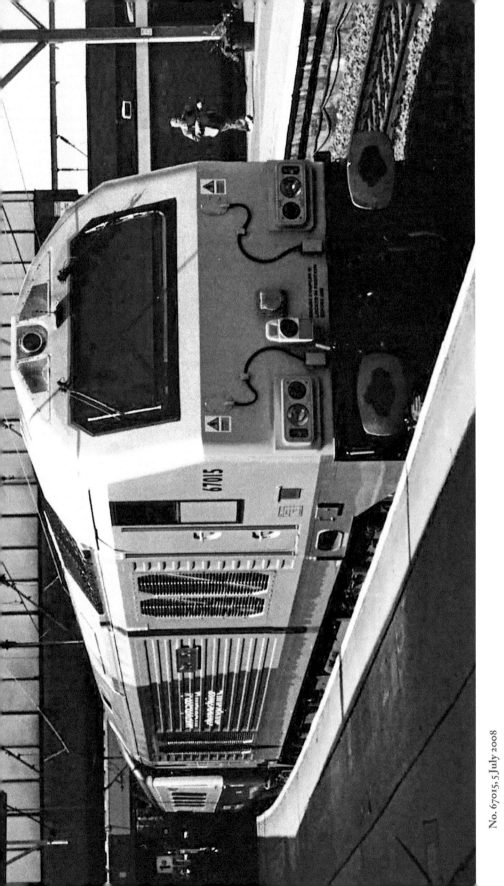

No. 67015, 5 July 2008

No. 67015 *David J. Lloyd* is seen at Wolverhampton while carrying Wrexham & Shropshire livery. This operation only lasted for a couple of years from 2008, with them being hampered by not being allowed to call at Birmingham New Street due to a Moderation of Competition clause in the Virgin Trains contract.

Bescot

No. 08623, 6 November 1999

No. 08623 (D3790) is seen on pilot duty at Bescot while carrying BR blue livery. This loco would go on to receive DB Cargo red livery, and would become the very last Class 08 to leave Bescot depot when it was removed by new owner Harry Needle in 2017, leaving Bescot without a Class 08 on site for the first time in over fifty years.

No. 08759, 26 December 1987

No. 08759 (D3927, No. 09106) spends Christmas 1987 stabled at Bescot. At this time, Bescot had a large allocation of locomotives, both shunters and main-line locomotives. Of note is the Research Department Class 31 No. 97203 behind. No. 08759 was rebuilt as No. 09106, and was the last Class 09 to be in use with DB Cargo.

No. 08888, 7 May 2015

No. 08888 (D4118) is seen stabled at Bescot in front of the depot's re-railing train. No. 08888 carries EWS maroon livery, and has also been fitted with remote control equipment, as indicated by the extra lights above the cab windows. The loco has since been preserved at the Kent & East Sussex Railway.

No. 20055, 2 April 1983

No. 20055 (D8055) is seen stabled at Bescot among other Class 20 locomotives. Bescot was another favourite place to visit, as there were always long lines of locomotives stabled, especially on a weekend. No. 20055 would be broken up by M. C. Metals, Glasgow, in 1995.

No. 20136, 27 December 1983

No. 20136 (D8136) rests for the weekend at Bescot. Bescot always used to supply locomotives for the many coal, Speedlink and engineers workings originating in the area. No. 20136 still carries its BR double arrow on the cabside, although most Class 20s had it moved to the first bonnet door. No. 20136 would be scrapped by M.C. Metals in 1991.

No. 20145, 27 August 1989

No. 20145 (D8145, No. 2019) is seen stabled at Bescot. This loco was always immediately recognisable at the time due to the fact that the running number was positioned low on the cab. No. 20145 would later pass to RFS, being renumbered 2019 in their fleet. It would spend many months awaiting scrapping at European Metal Recycling's yard at Kingsbury, before being scrapped in 2009.

No. 20301, 18 June 2013

No. 20301 (D8047, Nos 20047 and 2004) is seen at Bescot with a nuclear working from Crewe to Bridgewater, along with classmate No. 20308. No. 20301 carries the name *Max Joule 1958–1999*, and this view shows where the locomotive stabling sidings used to be, which are now covered over by the virtual ballast site.

No. 25244, 31 March 1986

No. 25244 (D7594) is seen stabled at Bescot. This was taken at the time when the Class 25 locomotives were nearing the end of their working lives, but they could still be found around Bescot. No. 25244 would be preserved at the Kent & East Sussex Railway.

No. 25266, 2 March 1985

No. 25266 (D7616) is seen at Bescot during the time when BR blue livery still reigned on the network. There were always large numbers of stabled locomotives to be found at Bescot on a weekend, from Class 20s through to Class 58s and AC electric locomotives.

No. 25326, 26 January 1985

No. 25326 (D7676) is seen, having been withdrawn, at Bescot. This loco was on its way to Swindon Works for scrapping, hence the tail lamp that has been fitted. Swindon would scrap No. 25326 in 1986.

No. 31238, 10 November 1991

No. 31238 (D5665) is seen stabled at Bescot while carrying recently applied Civil Engineers 'Dutch' livery. No. 31238 also carries a Crewe depot plaque of a cat, indicating it was based at the Cheshire depot at the time. The Class 31 to the left carries a Bescot saddle depot plaque.

No. 31308, 24 March 1991

No. 31308 (D5841) is seen stabled at Bescot, also carrying Civil Engineers 'Dutch' livery. By this time, the lines of Class 20s and Class 25s had given way to Class 31s as they were the staple motive power on departmental workings at the time.

No. 31403, 25 July 1993

No. 31403 (D5596) rests at Bescot while carrying BR blue livery alongside similar classmate No. 31415. Despite both locomotives carrying ETH equipment, their passenger working days were long gone, both having been relegated to engineers workings.

No. 31422, 24 May 1993

No. 31422 (D5844, Nos 31310 and 31522) is seen stabled at Bescot carrying InterCity Mainline livery. After its service career had finished, this loco ended up in use at Tyseley as a carriage-heating locomotive, before being finally scrapped by C. F. Booth, Rotherham, in 2014.

No. 37058, 21 February 1987

No. 37058 (D6758) is seen at Bescot, having been stabled for the weekend. Despite the large number of locos seen at Bescot, Class 37s were never that common when compared to the Class 31s and Class 47s. No. 37058 would be one of the Class 37s chosen to work in France on high-speed line construction trains, before being returned to the UK. It was scrapped by C. F. Booth, Rotherham, in 2009.

No. 37076, 8 February 1987

No. 37076 (D6776, No. 37518) is seen stabled at Bescot. The Class 37s that did visit Bescot for the weekend were normally based at Gateshead, with the South Wales-based locomotives being less common. No. 37076 would be rebuilt as No. 37518, and is today in use with West Coast Railways.

No. 37102, 12 April 1986

No. 37102 (D6802, No. 37712) shows signs of a rebuilt front end following collision damage. This unusual rebuild involved removing the headcode boxes, and the look gave a similar appearance to a refurbished loco. No. 37102 would become No. 37712 in the refurbishment programme, and is today based at Carnforth as a source of spares for the West Coast Railways fleet.

No. 37104, 9 March 1985

No. 37104 (D6804) stands at Bescot, surrounded by a fantastic assortment of other locomotives, including Class 20s, a Class 45, a Class 56 and a Class 86. This was a great time to visit Bescot, with such a variety of locomotives to see. No. 37104 would eventually be scrapped at Immingham in 2000.

No. 37217, 1 January 1985

No. 37217 (D6917, No. 97304) is seen at Bescot on New Year's Day 1985. This loco would spend many years stored at Ayr depot, before being bought by Network Rail, who refurbished it and returned it to service, renumbering it 97304.

No. 37238, 27 August 1989

No. 37238 (D6938) is seen at Bescot in front of a long line of stabled Class 47s. A Stratford Cockney Sparrow depot sticker can just be seen on the bodyside. No. 37238 would be scrapped by C. F. Booth, Rotherham, in 2009.

No. 43084, 25 April 1993

No. 43084 (No. 43484) works through Bescot, heading towards Birmingham New Street. It was unusual to see HSTs at Bescot, but the route was used as a diversion if the main line between Wolverhampton and Birmingham New Street was closed. No. 43084 carries the name *County of Derbyshire*, and also has buffers fitted from when it was used as a surrogate DVT with the East Coast Class 91 locomotives.

No. 45019, 27 October 1984

No. 45019 (D33) is seen stabled at Bescot along with another class member. The Class 45s were not seen in great numbers at Bescot, especially when compared to the Class 20s and Class 31s. No. 45019 would be withdrawn the following year, and was scrapped by Vic Berry, Leicester, in 1987.

No. 45033, 12 April 1986

No. 45033 (D39) stands at Bescot, awaiting its next turn of duty. This area is now where the virtual ballast site is, and there are very few locomotives stabled at Bescot nowadays. No. 45033 was scrapped by M. C. Metals, Glasgow, in 1992.

No. 47147, 13 June 1987

No. 47147 (D1740) is seen at Bescot while still carrying BR blue livery, along with the Class 20 and Class 56 seen in the background. No. 47147 would be another locomotive scrapped by Vic Berry, this time in 1999.

No. 47206, 21 February 1987
No. 47206 (D1856, No. 57605) is seen at Bescot, complete with snowploughs and Eastfield Scottie Dog depot sticker. This loco spent quite a few years allocated north of the border, and it was eventually rebuilt as No. 57605 for sleeper services on the Great Western.

No. 47207, 15 May 1994
No. 47207 (D1857) is seen at Bescot looking very scruffy. The scar on the side is where it has lost its *Bulmers of Hereford* nameplate. No. 47207 later passed to Freightliner, and would be scrapped by C. F. Booth, Rotherham, in 2005.

No. 47238, 9 October 1988

No. 47238 (D1915) is seen at Bescot station on the day it was named *Bescot Yard*. This was in connection with an open day held in the yard, and this was another place that always held a good display, due to the size of the yard.

No. 47367, 12 April 1993

No. 47367 (D1886) is seen at a very quiet Bescot while still carrying red stripe Railfreight livery. No. 47367 also carries the unofficial name *Kenny Cockbird*, as applied by Tinsley depot. This loco can today be found preserved at the Mid-Norfolk Railway.

No. 56035, 3 May 1986

No. 56035 *Taff Merthyr* is seen at Bescot while carrying recently applied original Railfreight livery. This loco was allocated to Cardiff Canton at the time, and it was unusual to see CF-allocated Class 56s on Bescot, with Toton-based locomotives being more common.

No. 56054, 5 June 1994

No. 56054 is another Cardiff-based Class 56 that was seen at Bescot. This loco carries Trainload Metals livery, and also the large *British Steel Llanwern* nameplate. The impressive Cardiff Canton Goat depot plaque is seen on the secondman's cabside.

No. 56065, 24 January 1987

No. 56065 approaches Bescot with a rake of two-axle cement wagons. At the time, No. 56065 carried original Railfreight livery, and the old steam shed can be seen in the background on the left. This was finally demolished in 2014.

No. 56093, 15 May 1994

No. 56093 rests in the yard at Bescot with another class member. No. 56093 carries unbranded Trainload Freight livery, and also the name *The Institution of Mining Engineers*. No. 56093 was one of the Class 56s that were stored for a couple of years at Healey Mills before being scrapped by European Metal Recycling, Attercliffe.

No. 56109, 11 April 1987

No. 56109 is seen at Bescot carrying large logo livery, complete with white window surrounds. The Class 56s were seen at Bescot as they were used on coal traffic to Ironbridge and Didcot. No. 56109 was scrapped by T. J. Thompson, Stockton, in 2011.

No. 58005, 2 February 1985

No. 58005 is seen between a pair of BR blue-liveried Class 56s at Bescot. Class 58s would also be in abundance at Bescot at weekends, again working coal trains to Ironbridge and Didcot, and also working out of Daw Mill Colliery. No. 58005 was sent abroad to work in France, and is today stored at Alizay, Rouen.

No. 60066, 27 February 2016

No. 60066, carrying a special Drax livery, is seen showing the modern-day scene at Bescot. The Class 60s are a bit scarce at Bescot today due to the small number that are in traffic.

No. 66214, 7 July 2014

No. 66214 is seen at Bescot while carrying Euro Cargo Rail livery. This is one of the Class 66s that EWS sent to work in France, and it is seen on its way to Toton for repairs before returning to the Continent. These locomotives are hauled when in the UK, rather than working under their own power.

No. 66721, 26 May 2015

No. 66721 *Harry Beck* is seen as an example of today's motive power at Bescot. These locomotives can be seen daily at Bescot, usually operating for all the major freight companies. No. 66721 is operated by GBRf, and carries a special London Transport Museum advert livery.

No. 67029, 16 July 2016

No. 67029 is seen stabled at Bescot while carrying its unique silver livery. It gained this livery to work with the EWS Executive Train in 2005, although this train is seldom seen working today. No. 67029 carries the name *Royal Diamond* to celebrate the Queen's diamond wedding anniversary.

No. 68013, 18 March 2015

No. 68013 represents another new class of locomotive seen at Bescot. This loco is operated by Direct Rail Services, and carries Chiltern Mainline livery as it is normally to be found working passenger services out of London Marylebone. Here, however, it is seen with a CWR train at Bescot.

No. 85003, 18 April 1987

No. 85003 (E3058, No. 85113) is seen at the south end of Bescot yard coupled with No. 87019 *Sir Winston Churchill*. Electric locomotives could also be found at Bescot, although in not as great a number as diesel locomotives. The vast majority of wagons in the background have been replaced and scrapped.

No. 85011, 22 March 1986

No. 85011 (E3066, No. 85114) spends the weekend stabled at Bescot. The AC electric locomotives were stabled at Bescot, ready to work Speedlink services out of the yard, and they could be found mixed in with stabled diesel locomotives due to not having any particular road to be stabled on.

No. 85015, 7 June 1987

No. 85015 (E3070) is seen at Bescot in the company of a BR blue-liveried Class 87, which were also used on freight services at this time. No. 85015 would be scrapped by M. C. Metals, Glasgow, in 1992.

No. 85036, 15 May 1988

No. 85036 (E3091, No. 85110) is seen at Bescot, stabled with unique Class 87 No. 87101 *Stephenson*. No. 85036 would go on to be renumbered 85110, and was another to be scrapped by M. C. Metals, Glasgow, in 1992.

No. 97406, 26 December 1986

No. 97406 (D335, No. 40135) is seen stabled in the Down yard at Bescot. This loco had been renumbered for departmental duties involving the Crewe remodelling work. By the time this shot was taken it had been withdrawn from service, and was on its way to Tyseley, from where it was subsequently preserved.

No. 304015, 26 August 1985

No. 304015 is seen departing Bescot with a service to Walsall. These services are today operated by Class 350 units, and the station has been rebuilt with wider platforms to cope with the larger number of passengers – especially when Walsall FC are playing, as their ground is now just behind the M6 motorway to the right.

No. 312203, 14 February 1987

No. 312203 (No. 312729) departs Bescot, heading for Birmingham New Street. There were four Class 312 units working in the West Midlands before they were transferred to East Ham, joining their other classmates. The stabling point can be seen in the background.

Rugeley

D9009, 5 July 2016

D9009 (No. 55009) *Alycidon* approaches Rugeley Trent Valley while hauling Class 40 D213 *Andania* towards Crewe. This shot goes to show that there are still some surprising scenes to be seen on the network today, despite its regular procession of multiple units.

No. 68006, 29 April 2016

No. 68006 *Daring* is seen waiting to pass through Rugeley Trent Valley with a rake of sleeper-carrying wagons. This locomotive is operated by Direct Rail Services, and carries Scotrail Saltire livery. These services normally operate from Bescot to Crewe via Bushbury and Portobello, but this one was diverted via Rugeley.

Birmingham

No. 47050, 27 August 1983

No. 47050 (D1632) passes Saltley depot while on West Coast Main Line electric drag duties, hauling No. 86245 towards Birmingham New Street from Nuneaton. This was a regular sight during this time, especially when the overhead wires were turned off between Birmingham and Rugby.

No. 66593, 3 February 2015

No. 66593 passes through Coleshill Parkway with a Freightliner service to Felixstowe. This is a relatively new station, only being open since 2007, and this view shows the current type of motive power seen on the majority of today's freight workings. No. 66593 carries the name *3MG Mersey Multimodal Gateway*.

No. 86401, 28 February 1991

No. 86401 (E3199, No. 86001) is seen at Birmingham New Street while carrying Network SouthEast livery and the name *Northampton Town*. This shot was taken at the time when there were still first generation DMUs to be seen at New Street, and before the second footbridge was installed, which further reduced the natural light in the station.

No. 20063, 26 July 1990

No. 20063 (D8063, No. 2002) passes Washwood Heath along with classmate No. 20145. This was a great place to watch comings and goings, being located on the busy stretch of line between Saltley and the Sutton Park line. No. 20063 was sold to CFD in France, and was renumbered 2002 in their fleet.

No. 20228, 10 June 1990

No. 20228 (D8128, No. 2004) is seen waiting to depart the RMC sleeper-manufacturing site at Washwood Heath. This view had changed very little over the years – the only major difference being that the chain link fence had been replaced with a modern high fence. No. 20228 was also sold to CFD in France, becoming No. 2004, but was preserved on its return to the UK, and is today based at the Barry Tourist Railway, South Wales.

No. 31446, 30 March 1990

No. 31446 (D5850, Nos 31316 and 31546) passes Washwood Heath with a London Underground train from Derby. These moves were quite common at the time, and can also be seen today, with new stock being delivered from Derby.

No. 31467, 23 May 1991

No. 31467 (D5641, No. 31216) passes the gasholders at Washwood Heath while carrying BR blue livery. Today, the gasholders have been dismantled and removed, and No. 31467 has also been dismantled (by European Metal Recycling, Kingsbury, in 2008).

No. 43123, 17 August 1993

No. 43123 (No. 43423) passes Washwood Heath while carrying InterCity Swallow livery, with buffers fitted. This was heading towards Birmingham New Street, and ultimately the South West. No. 43123 is today working for East Midlands Trains, while carrying Grand Central livery and the number 43423.

No. 47144, 11 March 1991

No. 47144 (D1737) propels a couple of TTA diesel tank wagons into the Metro-Cammell works at Washwood Heath. This was an unusual move at the time, as Class 156 production had finished a couple of years earlier, and the next diesel units built would be the Class 175s in 1999.

No. 47152, 13 September 1996

No. 47152 (D1745, No. 47398) pulls away from a signal check at Washwood Heath with a Freightliner working, heading for Southampton. This view shows the staple diet for Freightliner workings at the time, until the arrival of the Class 66s eradicated the vast majority of the Class 47s.

No. 47478, 26 February 1988

No. 47478 (D1608) passes Washwood Heath while still carrying BR blue livery. This loco would survive in use until 2000, retaining its blue livery to the end. It was scrapped by European Metal Recycling, Kingsbury, in 2006.

No. 47845, 23 July 1996

No. 47845 (D1653, Nos 47069, 47638 and 57301) *County of Kent* passes Washwood Heath with an InterCity working, heading towards Birmingham New Street. This shot was taken just prior to privatisation, and the Class 47s would eventually be replaced on these services by Class 220 Voyager units. No. 47845 was eventually rebuilt as No. 57301 for Virgin Trains West Coast.

No. 47971, 3 June 1991

No. 47971 (D1616, Nos 47480 and 97480) hauls two Mk 4 DVTs and a First Class Mk 4 FO from the nearby Metro-Cammell works to Bounds Green depot, London. These were regular moves at the time, delivering new stock and also returning stock for repairs. No. 47971 carries the name *Robin Hood*.

No. 60021, 13 September 1996

No. 60021 passes Washwood Heath light engine while carrying Trainload Metals livery and the name *Pen-y-ghent*. The Class 60s helped eliminate many of the older locomotives when they were introduced.

No. 66038, 22 January 1999

No. 66038 is seen at Washwood Heath when brand new. This view shows the current type of locomotive to be seen around Washwood Heath today, with examples from all the different freight operators to be seen.

No. 66305, 2 July 2008

No. 66305 is seen at an overgrown Washwood Heath while carrying Jarvis Fastline livery. Five Class 66s were delivered to this operator, but they passed to Direct Rail Services after only two years of service.

No. 66507, 1 August 2000

No. 66507 is seen, when only six weeks old, at Washwood Heath at the head of a Jarvis track renewals train. These trains carried newly built sleepers from the RMC factory at Washwood Heath to various parts of the country. Today, Network Rail operates these wagons.

No. 67026, 20 December 2001

No. 67026 passes Washwood Heath on a working it was built for – a Royal Mail Parcels service. EWS would eventually lose the Royal Mail contract in 2003, meaning these locomotives were relegated to more mundane duties, but their high speed and ETH equipment make them ideal for charter traffic.

No. 156513, 20 September 1989

No. 156513 is seen while out on test from the Metro-Cammell factory. This was the penultimate Class 156 built, and would soon head off to Corkerhill depot, Glasgow, to start service. The Strathclyde Transport livery suited this class of unit well.

Water Orton

No. 8180, 19 September 1973

No. 8180 (No. 20180) passes through Water Orton with a rake of Blue Circle cement Presflo wagons. Despite being over forty years ago, this view at Water Orton hasn't changed too much; the only major difference is that the line the Class 20 is seen on has since been lifted, meaning there is only one line on that side of the platform today.

No. 37602, 30 May 2017

No. 37602 (D6782, Nos 37082 and 37502) works through Water Orton, along with classmate No. 37606, on a Bescot to Toton engineers service. This view shows how overgrown the trees have become in the years since the previous shot.

No. 43156, 13 June 1995

No. 43156 passes Water Orton, heading towards Birmingham New Street. Water Orton is a must for any visiting enthusiast in the Midlands as it is a very busy junction where the lines to Derby and Leicester split. In the other direction, the Sutton Park freight-only line splits from the main line towards Birmingham and the South West.

No. 47485, 19 March 1987

No. 47485 (D1683) approaches Water Orton with a northbound passenger working consisting solely of Mk 1 carriages. This view was taken just south of the station, but this spot is obscured by a high fence today.

No. 58032, 19 March 1987

No. 58032 approaches Water Orton with a light engine move from the nearby Saltley depot. Today, No. 58032 is another member of the class to be found stored at Alizay, Rouen, in northern France.

No. 70805, 19 November 2014

No. 70805 passes Water Orton at the head of a quad Class 70 working from Westbury to Bescot. The other locomotives are Nos 70806, 70809 and 70810, and all work for Colas Rail Freight. This is a daily working, and is a nice change of motive power from the usual Class 66 locomotives found at Water Orton today.

Rugby

No. 47150, 6 June 1997

No. 47150 (D1743, No. 47399) passes the former signal box at Rugby with a northbound Freightliner working. This loco carries an unusual grey livery, but was scrapped by T. J. Thompson, Stockton, in 2010 while carrying Freightliner green livery.

No. 47840, 5 July 2004

No. 47840 (D1661, Nos 47077 and 47613) *North Star* is seen in one of the north bays at Rugby while carrying BR blue livery. The loco had been repainted into this livery towards the end of its Virgin Trains career, and has today been preserved at the West Somerset Railway. This shot was taken before Rugby was rebuilt; the two north bays are no longer used, and have been filled in.

No. 66127, 12 September 2015

No. 66127 pauses at Rugby with an engineers working. This view shows Rugby today, with the new Network Rail signalling control centre in the background. Rugby is still busy for freight, although the motive power is normally in the form of Class 66s and Class 90s.

No. 81002, 10 August 1982

No. 81002 (E3003) passes through Rugby while hauling a Class 304 electric unit. This shot was taken at a time when the early AC electric fleet was still in abundance, with only the Class 84s having been taken out of service. No. 81002 was eventually preserved, and is today housed at Barrow Hill.

No. 86259, 14 June 2017

No. 86259 (E3137, No. 86045) *Les Ross* is seen stabled round the back of Rugby station alongside newcomer No. 88002 *Prometheus*. This view is taken from Platform 6, which was only built in 2008. This view shows two different generations of West Coast Main Line AC locomotives, but it remains to be seen if the Class 88s will stay around as long as No. 86259.

No. 92038, 28 April 2015

No. 92038 is seen on test at Rugby, having just been released from overhaul for Caledonian Sleeper services, including a repaint into Caledonian livery. Classmate No. 92018 is seen behind in a similar condition. No. 92038 originally carried the name *Voltaire*.

No. 310113, 6 June 1997

No. 310113 (No. 310065) is seen stabled in one of the north bays at Rugby while carrying Regional Railways livery. This was one of thirteen Class 310 units renumbered for West Midlands services, and all were withdrawn by 2002. Since this shot was taken, the impressive roof at Rugby has been removed and the bays at this end have been filled in, being no longer in use.

No. 319001, 6 June 1997

No. 319001 is seen in one of the south bays at Rugby, waiting to depart for Brighton. This was an innovative service, but unfortunately it didn't survive in this form for long. A similar service is operated by Southern today, starting at Milton Keynes Central but only going as far as East Croydon.

Northampton

No. 08543, 10 March 1996

No. 08543 (D3707) is seen acting as a station pilot at Northampton. On this day there were two Class 08s on duty at Northampton – No. 08927 being the other. No. 08543 has since been scrapped by European Metal Recycling, Kingsbury, in 2010.

No. 56312, 3 June 2016

No. 56312 (No. 56003) *Jeremiah Dixon* is seen running light engine through Northampton, heading for Willesden. Northampton is the furthest south you can travel on a West Midlands day ranger, and is also a busy station, with passenger services for London and Birmingham, and also the majority of West Coast Main Line freight workings passing through the station.

No. 66108, 6 September 2012

No. 66108 represents the motive power used on the vast majority of freight passing through Northampton today. It is seen hauling a rake of Continental-registered Cargowaggons south.

No. 66955, 3 June 2016

No. 66955 heads north through Northampton with a Felixstowe to Lawley Street (Birmingham) Freightliner service. There are a large number of these services passing through Northampton on a daily basis.

Hereford

No. 60005, 30 May 1993

No. 60005 *Skiddaw* is seen at Hereford while hauling a special passenger working in connection with the joint open days held at Shrewsbury and Hereford on the same day. Twenty-five years later, the station at Hereford has hardly changed.

No. 67001, 13 August 2013

No. 67001 arrives at Hereford with an Arriva Trains Wales service from Holyhead to Cardiff Central. Hereford is the furthest west the West Midlands day ranger can take you.